HELLO
FUNGI

LAURENCE KING

LAURENCE KING
First published in Great Britain in 2023
by Laurence King

HB ISBN 978-1-51023-045-3
E-book ISBN 978-1-51023-079-8

10 9 8 7 6 5 4 3 2 1

Printed in China

MIX
Paper from
responsible sources
FSC® C104740

Natural history consultants: Sarah Niemann and Derek Niemann

Laurence King
An imprint of
Hachette Children's Group
Part of Hodder and Stoughton
Carmelite House
50 Victoria Embankment
London EC4Y 0DZ

An Hachette UK Company
www.hachette.co.uk
www.hachettechildrens.co.uk
www.laurenceking.com

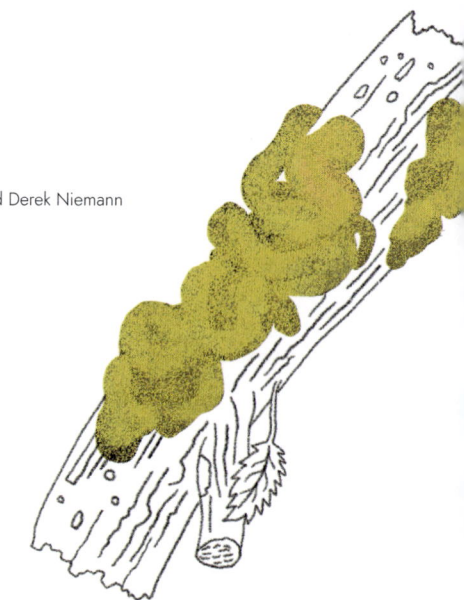

Nina Chakrabarti

HELLO FUNGI

A Little Guide to Nature

LAURENCE KING

CONTENTS

*We know more about the
movement of celestial bodies
than about the soil underfoot.*

Leonardo da Vinci

It is fun to spot fungi out in the wild,
but do not ever touch or pick mushrooms.
Many are poisonous to humans.

WHAT are FUNGI?

Fungi are not plants, nor are they animals.
They are a huge kingdom of simple living organisms.

MUSHROOMS are the fruit
of a much larger fungus
that grows underground.

This underground part of the
fungus is called MYCELIUM.

Mushrooms reproduce by making SPORES. They are so tiny you may not be able to see them.

Mycelium is made up of tiny threads called HYPHAE. It looks like a huge tangle of very thin string.

TINY FUNGI

Let's take a look at three types of microscopic* fungi.

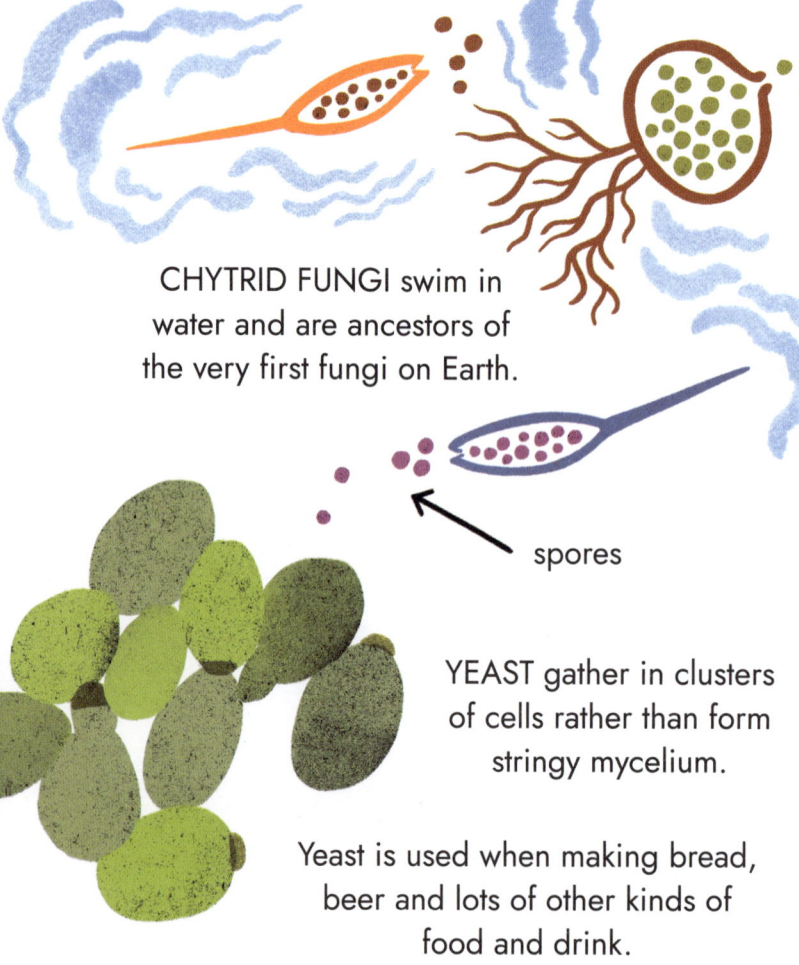

CHYTRID FUNGI swim in water and are ancestors of the very first fungi on Earth.

spores

YEAST gather in clusters of cells rather than form stringy mycelium.

Yeast is used when making bread, beer and lots of other kinds of food and drink.

* So small that you would need a microscope to see them.

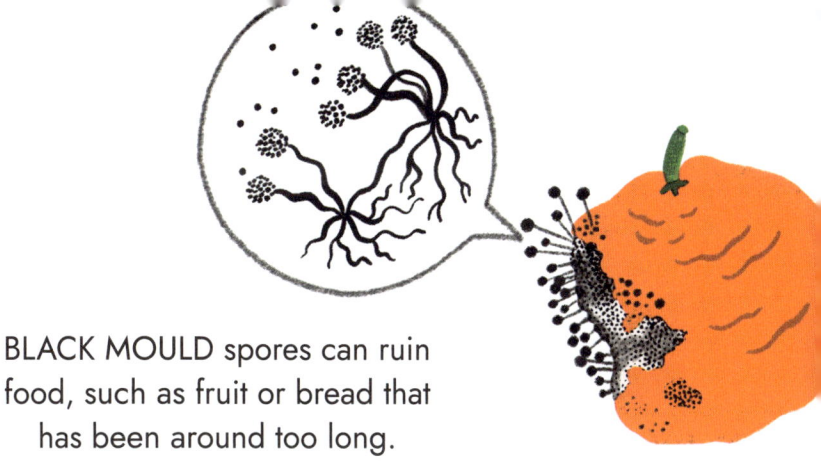

BLACK MOULD spores can ruin food, such as fruit or bread that has been around too long.

A BLUE MOULD called *penicillium roqueforti* is used to make blue cheese. It is safe to eat, and some people find it tasty!

Some GREEN MOULD is good at killing harmful bacteria.

Penicillium chrysogenum has given us a very useful medicine called penicillin. It is used to fight infections.

HELPFUL FUNGI

MYCORRHIZAL fungi are Earth's hidden helpers.

They form a giant underground network
connecting the roots of trees and plants
to the water and nutrients they need to grow.

The network acts like an information superhighway, sending chemical signals back and forth between trees and plants.

Ninety percent of all plant life on Earth depends on mycorrhizal fungi to survive.

THE DECOMPOSERS

SAPROPHYTIC fungi feasts on dead and decaying
plant and animal remains.

OAK-LEAF PINWHEEL
Gymnopus quercophilus

The Oak-leaf Pinwheel eats dead oak leaves.

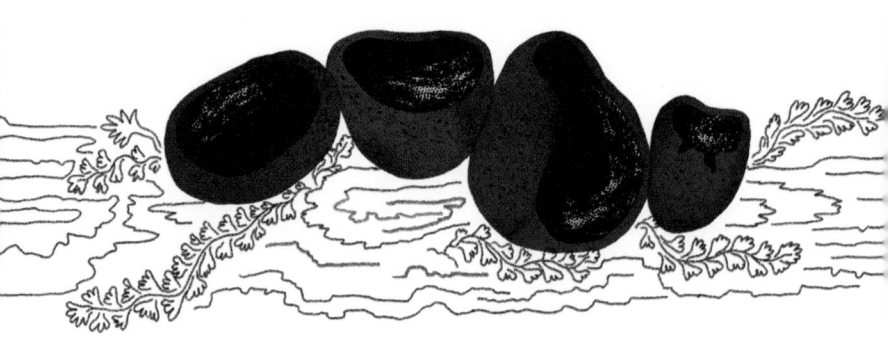

BLACK BULGAR
Bulgaria inquinans

Black Bulgar eats the
rotting wood of fallen trees.

There are many types of saprophytic fungi.
It is the largest group in the fungi kingdom.

This fungus feeds
on fallen pine cones.

PINECONE MUSHROOM
Auriscalpium vulgare

Saprophytic fungi help the environment
by recycling rotting and dead material
and releasing good nutrients into the soil.

GILL and SAC FUNGI

Gill fungi produce spores from gills — the pretty, delicate folds under the cap.

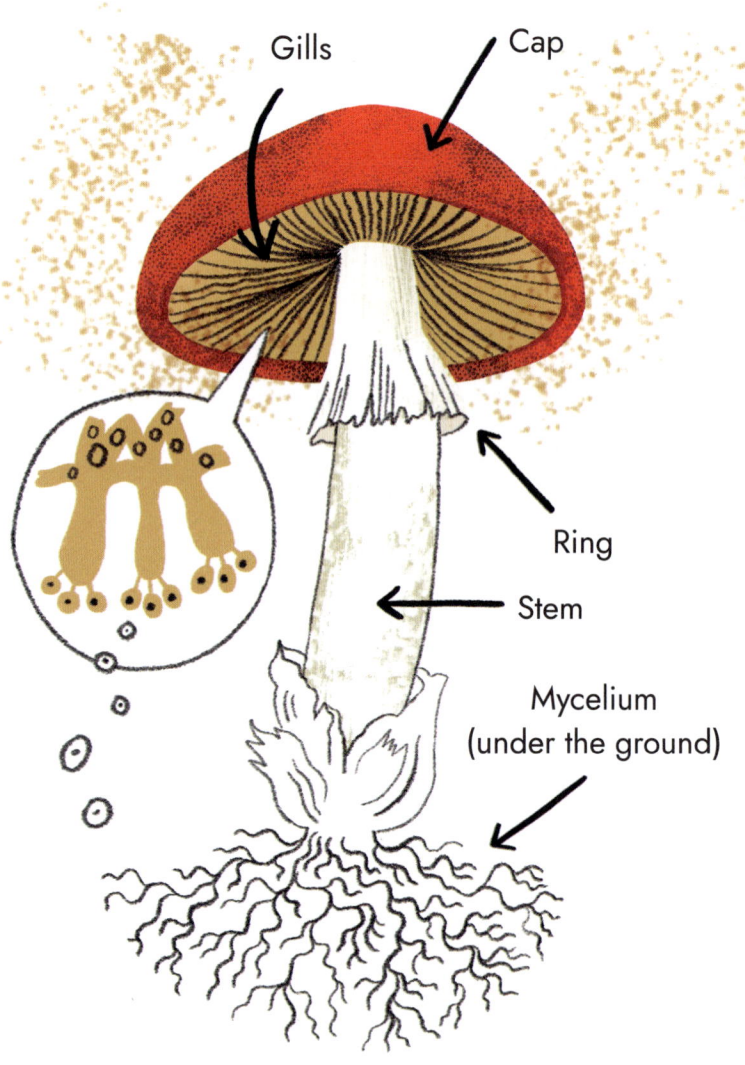

Gills

Cap

Ring

Stem

Mycelium
(under the ground)

Sac or cup fungi create spores inside
their amazing cup-shaped bodies.

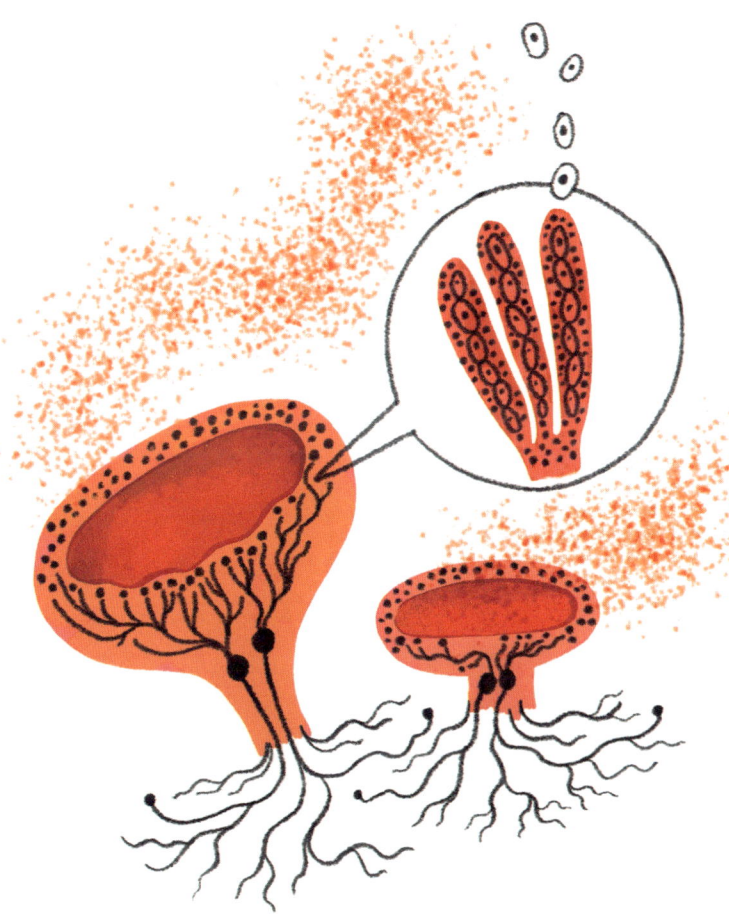

Millions of spores pour out of gill and sac
fungi and gently waft away in the wind.

PORE FUNGI

BOLETES and POLYPORES have miniscule holes called pores on the underside of their caps.

Behind each pore is a tiny tube.

BUTTER-FOOT BOLETE
Boletus auripes

Most POLYPORES or bracket fungi spring out of tree trunks and rotting wood, although some grow on soil.

Spores are produced in the tubes and pour out in their millions.

SHAGGY BRACKET
Inonotus hispidus

FUNGAL SPORES

Fungi produce millions of spores that come in all different shapes, sizes and colours.

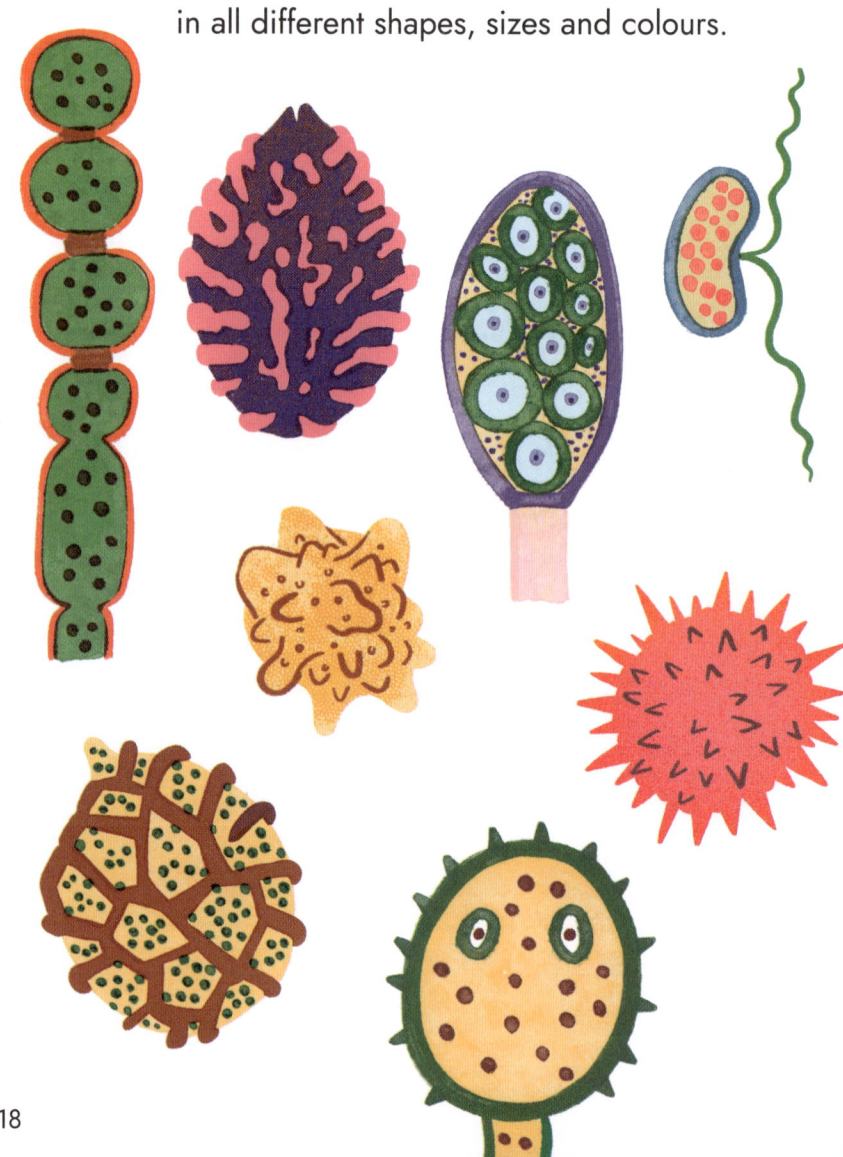

These spores are tiny. Under a microscope they look like weird alien creatures!

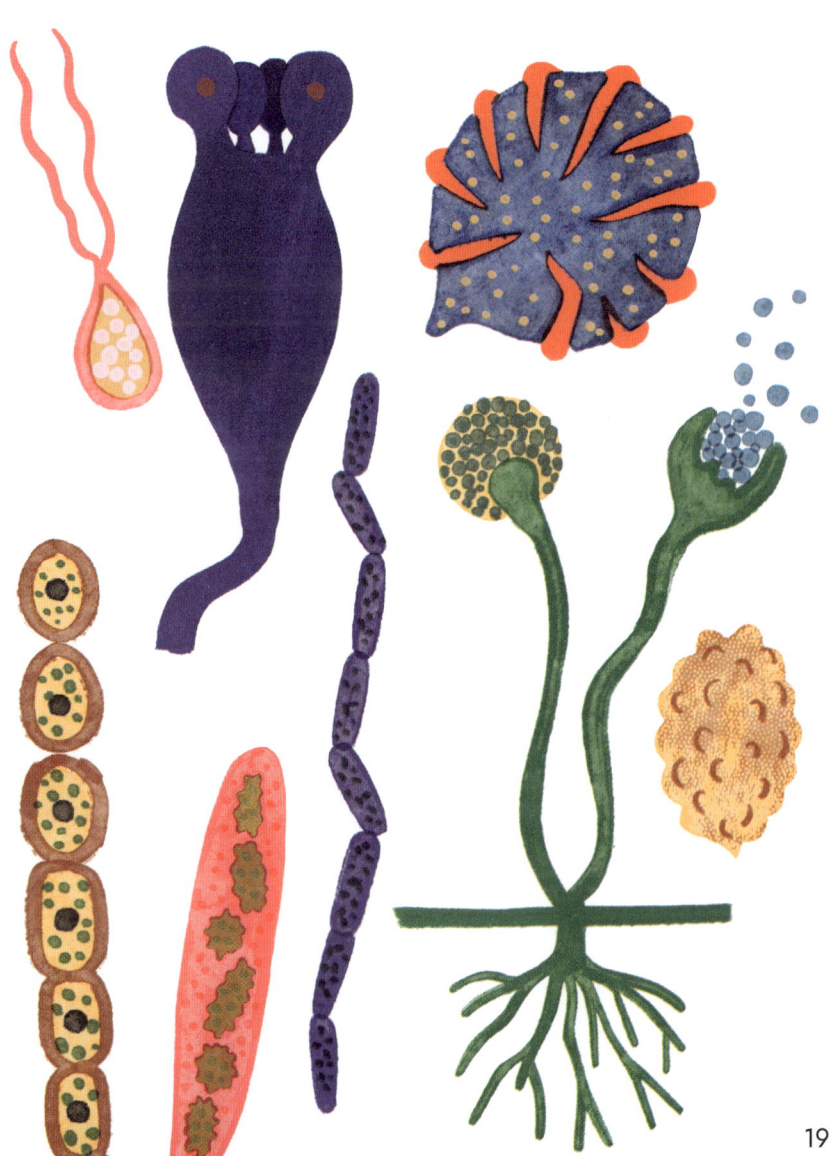

MAKE a SPORE PRINT

ALWAYS USE STORE-BOUGHT MUSHROOMS

You will need:

* Mushrooms
* Paper or card
* A bowl

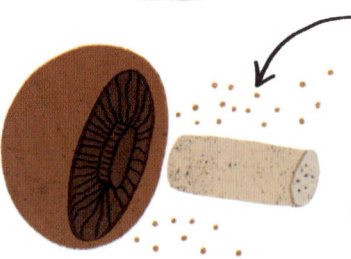

SPORES FALL FROM THE GILLS

1. Remove the stem, taking care not to damage the delicate gills.

2. Place the mushroom cap onto paper and cover with a bowl.

3. Leave for six hours or longer, then lift the bowl and the mushroom off the paper to reveal your spore print.

SHOOTING SPORES

Fungi spread their spores in imaginative ways.

COMMON BIRD'S-NEST
Crucibulum laeve

These fungi are filled with tiny 'eggs' or spore sacks.
When splashed by rain, the sacks explode
and spores spring high into the air.

WOLF FART
Lycoperdon perlatum

ARCHED EARTHSTAR
Geastrum fornicatum

THE HITCH-HIKERS

Cordyceps and Ophiocordyceps fungi grow on the bodies of insects. These types of fungi are called parasites.

ZOMBIE-ANT FUNGUS
Ophiocordyceps unilateralis

BEETLE FUNGUS
Ophiocordyceps entomorrhiza

There are thousands of different types of parasitic fungi. They each choose a particular insect to infect.

Parasitic fungi keep the insect population from getting too large and help maintain a harmonious balance in nature.

SCARLET CATERPILLAR FUNGUS
Cordyceps militaris

Silky Piggyback is a fungus that grows on other fungi.
This parasite does not harm its host.

SILKY PIGGYBACK
Asterophora parasitica

SMELLY FUNGI

Stinkhorn fungi are very smelly.

DOG STINKHORN
Mutinus caninus

The horrible smell* attracts flies and other insects that nibble at the slimy material produced by the fungi.

ANEMONE STINKHORN
Aseroe rubra

* Disgusting to us, delicious to insects!

SUBTERRANEAN* FUNGI

Truffles are a fungi that grow underground.
They like growing near oak, hazel and beech trees.

Truffles use a delicious scent to tempt animals to
dig them up, eat and distribute their spores.

* 'Subterranean' means under the ground.

decaying log

People like to eat truffles too, and use specially
trained dogs or pigs to sniff them out!

EDIBLE FUNGI

All kinds of tasty fungi can be found
in shops and markets.

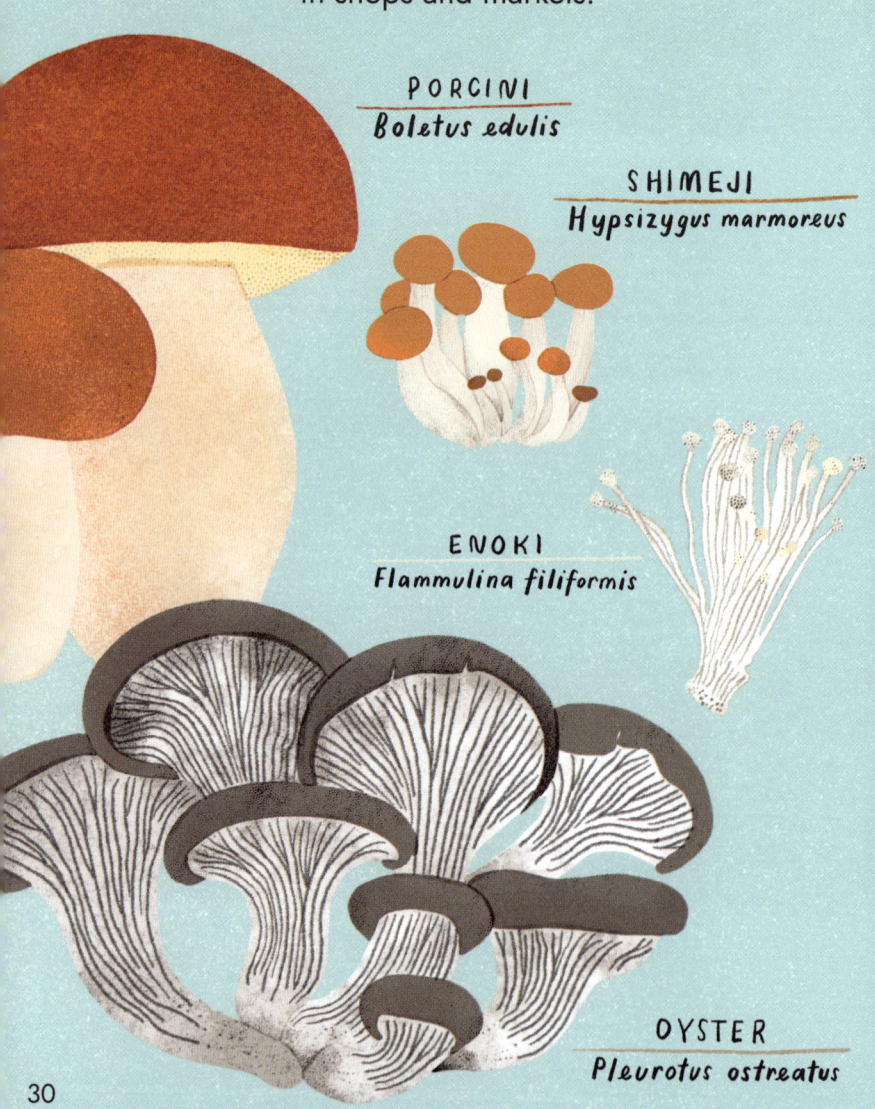

PORCINI
Boletus edulis

SHIMEJI
Hypsizygus marmoreus

ENOKI
Flammulina filiformis

OYSTER
Pleurotus ostreatus

PORTOBELLO
Agaricus bisporus

MATSUTAKE
Tricholoma matsutake

CHANTERELLE
Cantharellus cibarius

Have you eaten any of these?

31

MUSHROOMS on TOAST

Ingredients:

* ✳ 500g chestnut or mixed mushrooms,*
  cleaned and sliced
* ✳ 2 cloves of garlic, finely chopped
* ✳ A knob of butter or splash of olive oil
* ✳ Parsley, roughly chopped
* ✳ Toast and butter to serve!

*Some mushrooms in the wild are very poisonous,
so only ever use those you have bought in a shop.

Method:

Ask an adult to help you.

1. Heat a pan and put in the butter or olive oil.

2. Fry the mushrooms on a low heat until they are soft.

3. Add the garlic and fry until cooked (around 3 to 4 minutes).

4. Add the chopped parsley and serve on the hot, buttered toast.

Delicious!

COLOURFUL FUNGI

Fungi grow around the world,
and in all colours of the rainbow.

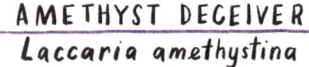

AMETHYST DECEIVER
Laccaria amethystina

SKY-BLUE MUSHROOM
Entoloma hochstetteri

SCARLET ELF CUP
Sarcoscypha austriaca

WITCHES' BUTTER
Tremella mesenterica

ORANGE PORE FUNGUS
Favolaschia calocera

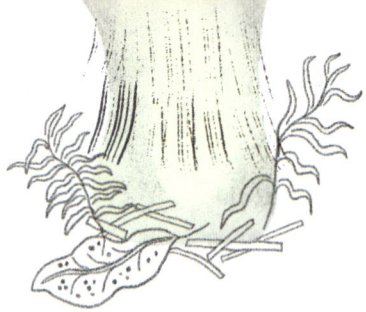

FLY AGARIC
Amanita muscaria

VIOLET CORAL
Clavaria zollingeri

WEIRD and WONDERFUL

This fungus looks like it's dripping ink.

SHAGGY INKCAP
Coprinus comatus

The black inky liquid
is filled with spores.

Look out for the Shaggy Inkcap on lawns,
along roads and near drains.

And this one looks just like a brain!

FALSE MOREL
Gyromitra esculenta

True morels have hollow insides and
false morels have a soft tissue interior.

STRANGE and CURIOUS

This strange fungus looks like it is bleeding.

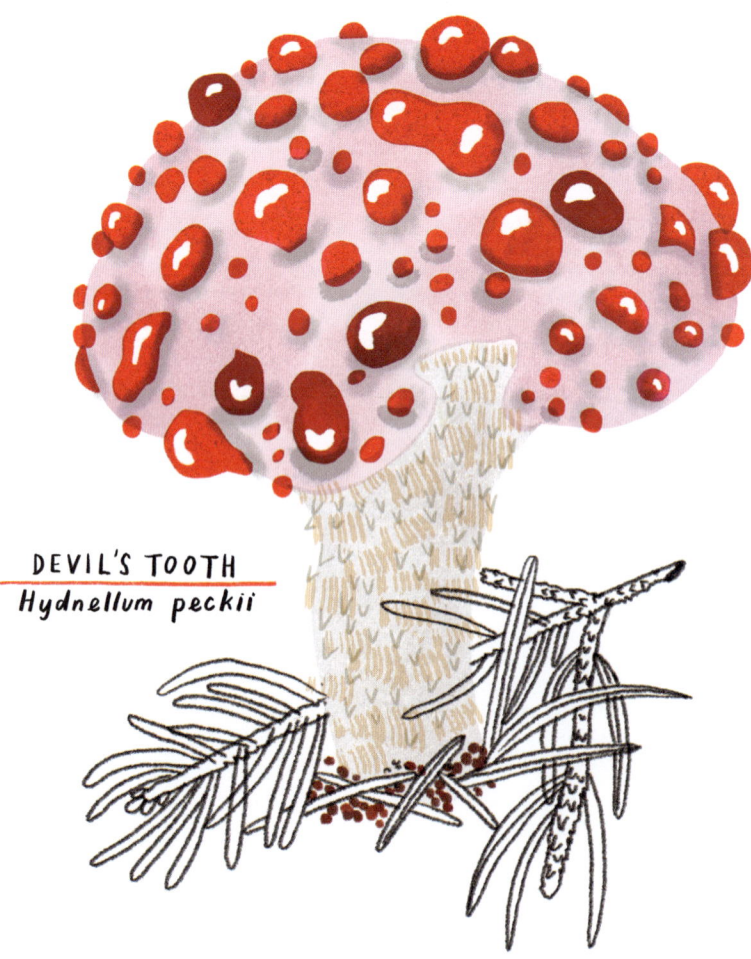

DEVIL'S TOOTH
Hydnellum peckii

The rarely seen Devil's Tooth grows near pine trees.

This one looks
like it has teeth!

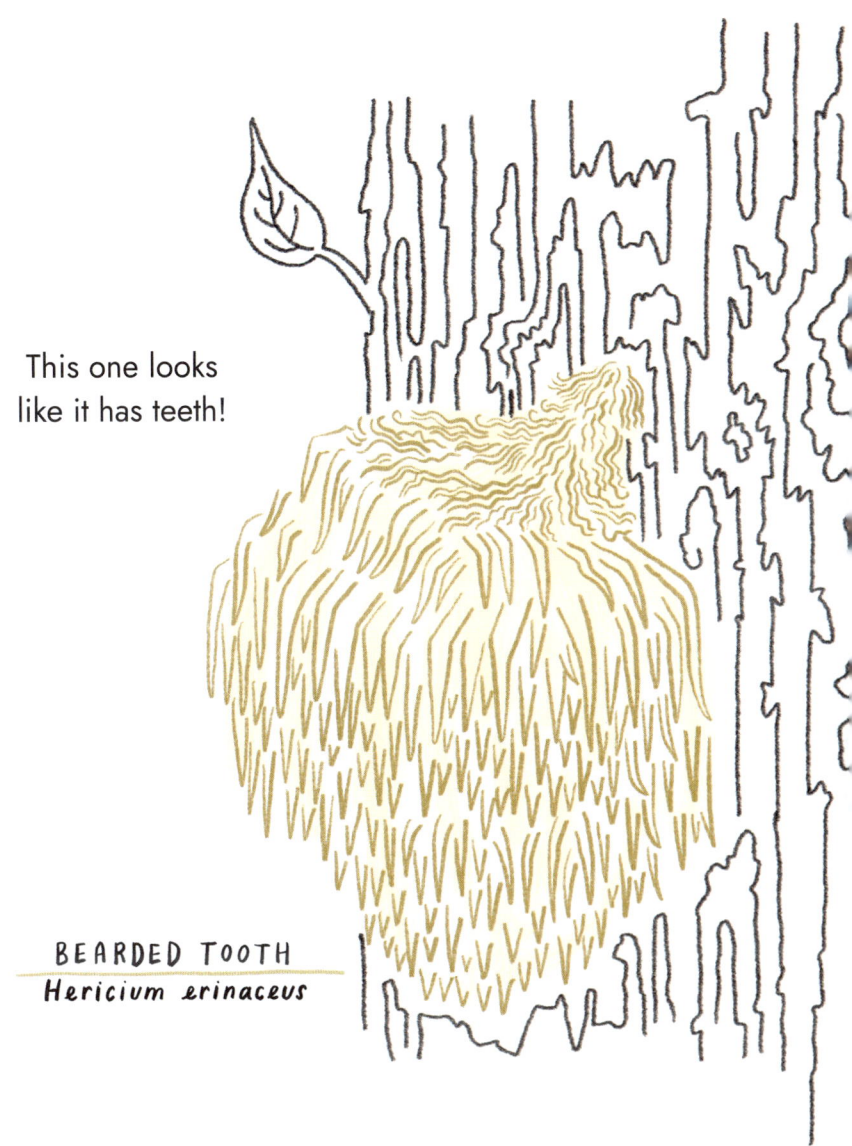

BEARDED TOOTH
Hericium erinaceus

Bearded Tooth mushrooms have been used in
Chinese medicine for hundreds of years.

DEADLY FUNGI

These fungi are poisonous to humans.

LOOK
BUT DO NOT
TOUCH!

DEVIL'S BOLETE
Rubroboletus satanas

FUNERAL BELL
Galerina marginata

DEATH CAP
Amanita phalloides

FOOL'S CONECAP
Conocybe filaris

DEADLY DAPPERLING
Lepiota brunneoincarnata

PANTHER CAP
Amanita pantherina

GLOW-in-the-DARK FUNGI

Some mushrooms can make their own light.
This is called bioluminescence.

GREEN PEPE
Mycena chlorophos

PIGEON FIRE
Mycena lux-coeli

ETERNAL LIGHT
Mycena luxaeterna

There are dozens of bioluminescent
species of fungi worldwide.

Scientists are not sure why they glow in the dark. It may be to attract nocturnal insects, who help to spread the fungi's spores. It's all about the spores!

PING-PONG BATS
Panellus pusillus

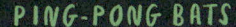

JACK-O'-LANTERN
Omphalotus olearius

LIGHT TREE DWELLER
Mycena luxarboricola

FUNGI IN FOLKLORE

A fairy ring is a circle of mushrooms, often growing in woodland.

In folklore, fairy rings are where fairies, elves and witches come to dance at night.

We now know that fairy rings
are caused by mycelium
growing outwards in a circle.

When mushrooms pop up, often after
rainfall, they do so at the edge of the circle.
The older the mycelium, the bigger the fairy ring.

FUNGI in HISTORY

In ancient EGYPT, mushrooms were thought to make you live forever. Only pharaohs were allowed to eat them.

Mushrooms appear in Egyptian art as far back as 4,500 years ago.

In 17th century JAPAN, tiny carvings called Netsuke were often shaped like mushrooms. They represented good fortune.

In early MAYAN and AZTEC cultures, mushrooms were thought to have been sent to Earth by lightning.

Mushroom statue from Guatemala

BE A FRIEND TO FUNGI

1. DO stop to take a good look, draw, paint and photograph any mushrooms you find.

2. DON'T touch or pick up fungi in the wild. It takes years of experience and knowledge to know which fungi are safe for humans.

3. LEAVE dead trees and fallen branches to decompose slowly and at their own pace. This is what feeds fungi!

4. TAKE CARE not to kick or tread on fungi when out and about in the wild.

5. FIND OUT all you can about fungi — there's still so much to discover and learn!